The Wood End Series

Stage 1

Teacher's Support Book

and

Precision Reading Programme

Written by Isabel Reynolds OCR Dip.SpLD

Illustrated By Jess Hart

www.fast-print.net/store.php

The Wood End Series - Stage 1
Teacher's Support Book and Precision Reading Programme

ISBN: 978-178035-619-8

All characters are fictional.
Any similarity to any actual person is purely coincidental.

A catalogue record for this book is available from the British Library

First published 2013 by
FASTPRINT PUBLISHING
Peterborough, England.

Introduction and Rationale
Wood End Scheme

Although there is no doubt that children with dyslexia or other reading difficulties need a structured phonic programme, for some this alone is not enough.
The Wood End Scheme and Precision Reading Programme should be used alongside a phonic programme. It focuses on the high frequency words in order of frequency.

Children who reach Key Stage 2 and are still unable to read are often faced with books which have been written for much younger children. This does nothing for their self esteem and certainly does little to encourage enjoyment of reading. There are reading schemes available which are low ability, high interest, but these, inevitably, still have many words which the child cannot read.

The Wood End Scheme is a completely new approach. Each stage is a story written in 8 or 9 short chapters.
Each chapter introduces a small number of new High Frequency Words which are printed in bold.
Two copies of each text is needed, one for the adult and one for the learner. The adult reads the story and the learner follows, (this will aid tracking as well). The learner reads all the words which are printed in bold.
There are also 1 or 2 comprehension questions at the end of each chapter.
The Precision Reading Programme should be used alongside the Wood End series to re-enforce the words being learnt.
The Connect games can further re-enforce the learning.

Before reading a new chapter the child should read the words covered in the previous chapter to recap before being introduced to the 'new' words.

Wood End Stage 1 Precision Reading Programme
First 100 high frequency words

Stage 1 - Read the 5 words
Stage 2 - Read the words in the grid correctly within 1 minute.
Stage 3 - 1 week later revisit the 5 words
Stage 4 - 1 month later revisit the 5 words.

and
a
to
said
the

and	to	a	to	and
and	a	to	said	the
the	to	the	the	and
said	a	and	a	said
to	said	said	to	and
the	said	a	the	a
and	to	a	to	and
and	a	to	said	the
the	to	the	the	and
said	a	and	a	said
to	said	said	to	and
the	said	a	the	a

GOAL! ------------------------------ 1minute with no mistakes

Precision Reading

Stage 1 - Read the 5 words

Stage 2 - Read the words in the grid correctly within 1 minute.

Stage 3 - 1 week later revisit the 5 words

Stage 4 - 1 month later revisit the 5 words.

in
he
I
of
it

in	I	he	I	in
in	he	I	of	it
it	I	it	it	in
of	he	in	he	of
I	of	of	I	in
it	of	he	it	he
in	I	he	I	in
in	he	I	of	it
it	I	it	it	in
of	he	in	he	of
I	of	of	I	in
it	of	he	it	he

GOAL! ------------------------------ 1minute with no mistakes

Precision Reading

Stage 1 – Read the 5 words

Stage 2 – Read the words in the grid correctly within 1 minute.

Stage 3 – 1 week later revisit the 5 words

Stage 4 – 1 month later revisit the 5 words.

was
you
they
on
she

was	they	you	they	was
was	you	they	on	she
she	they	she	she	was
on	you	was	you	on
they	on	on	they	was
she	on	you	she	you
was	they	you	they	was
was	you	they	on	she
she	they	she	she	was
on	you	was	you	on
they	on	on	they	was
she	on	you	she	you

GOAL! ------------------------------ 1minute with no mistakes

Precision Reading

Stage 1 - Read the 5 words

Stage 2 - Read the words in the grid correctly within 1 minute.

Stage 3 - 1 week later revisit the 5 words

Stage 4 - 1 month later revisit the 5 words.

but
his
at
for
is

but	at	his	at	but
but	his	at	for	is
is	at	is	is	but
for	his	but	his	for
at	for	for	at	but
is	for	his	is	his
but	at	his	at	but
but	his	at	for	is
is	at	is	is	but
for	his	but	his	for
at	for	for	at	but
is	for	his	is	his

GOAL! ------------------------------ 1minute with no mistakes

Precision Reading

Stage 1 - Read the 5 words

Stage 2 - Read the words in the grid correctly within 1 minute.

Stage 3 - 1 week later revisit the 5 words

Stage 4 - 1 month later revisit the 5 words.

white
three
six
red
five

white	six	three	six	white
white	three	six	six	five
five	red	five	five	white
six	three	white	three	red
red	six	six	six	white
five	red	three	five	three
white	six	three	six	white
white	three	red	red	five
five	red	five	five	white
six	three	white	three	six
red	red	six	red	white
five	six	three	five	three

GOAL! ------------------------------ 1minute with no mistakes

Precision Reading

Stage 1 - Read the 5 words

Stage 2 - Read the words in the grid correctly within 1 minute.

Stage 3 - 1 week later revisit the 5 words

Stage 4 - 1 month later revisit the 5 words.

can
we
all
with
that

can	all	we	all	can
can	we	all	with	that
that	all	that	that	can
with	we	can	we	with
all	with	with	all	can
that	with	we	that	we
can	all	we	all	can
can	we	all	with	that
that	all	that	that	can
with	we	can	we	with
all	with	with	all	can
that	with	we	that	we

GOAL! ------------------------------ 1minute with no mistakes

Precision Reading

Stage 1 - Read the 5 words

Stage 2 - Read the words in the grid correctly within 1 minute.

Stage 3 - 1 week later revisit the 5 words

Stage 4 - 1 month later revisit the 5 words.

her
my
had
up
are

her	had	my	had	her
her	my	had	up	are
are	had	are	are	her
up	my	her	my	up
had	up	up	had	her
are	up	my	are	my
her	had	my	had	her
her	my	had	up	are
are	had	are	are	her
up	my	her	my	up
had	up	up	had	her
are	up	my	are	my

GOAL! ------------------------------ 1minute with no mistakes

Precision Reading

Stage 1 - Read the 5 words

Stage 2 - Read the words in the grid correctly within 1 minute.

Stage 3 - 1 week later revisit the 5 words

Stage 4 - 1 month later revisit the 5 words.

this
out
have
there
what

this	have	out	have	this
this	out	have	there	what
what	have	what	what	this
there	out	this	out	there
have	there	there	have	this
what	there	out	what	out
this	have	out	have	this
this	out	have	there	what
what	have	what	what	this
there	out	this	out	there
have	there	there	have	this
what	there	out	what	out

GOAL! ------------------------------ 1minute with no mistakes

Precision Reading

Stage 1 – Read the 5 words

Stage 2 – Read the words in the grid correctly within 1 minute.

Stage 3 – 1 week later revisit the 5 words

Stage 4 – 1 month later revisit the 5 words.

some
like
be
went
so

some	be	like	be	some
some	like	be	went	so
so	be	so	so	some
went	like	some	like	went
be	went	went	be	some
so	went	like	so	like
some	be	like	be	some
some	like	be	went	so
so	be	so	so	some
went	like	some	like	went
be	went	went	be	some
so	went	like	so	like

GOAL! ----------------------------- 1minute with no mistakes

Precision Reading

Stage 1 - Read the 5 words

Stage 2 - Read the words in the grid correctly within 1 minute.

Stage 3 - 1 week later revisit the 5 words

Stage 4 - 1 month later revisit the 5 words.

one
I'm
six
black
two

one	six	I'm	six	one
one	I'm	six	black	two
two	six	two	two	one
black	I'm	one	I'm	black
six	black	black	six	one
two	black	I'm	two	I'm
one	six	I'm	six	one
one	I'm	six	black	two
two	six	two	two	one
black	I'm	one	I'm	black
six	black	black	six	one
two	black	I'm	two	I'm

GOAL! ------------------------------ 1minute with no mistakes

Precision Reading Record

Date	AM	PM	Words Correct	Comments

Connect for High Frequency Words

The Connect game boards can be photocopied and laminated. The games are for 2 players. Each player will need a set of counters.
In turn each player chooses a word to read. If they read it correctly they can place one of their counters over it. The winner is the first person to have four counters in a row.

The game boards can also be used for spelling. Each player needs a pencil and paper. In turn they select a word, read it, cover it and try to spell it. If it is spelt correctly they can cover it with a counter.

Connect For High Frequency Words

Wood End Stage 1

Game 1

the	and	a	to
said	in	he	I
of	it	was	you
they	on	she	is
for	at	his	but
that	with	all	we

Connect For High Frequency Words
Wood End Stage 1

Game 2

can	are	up	had
my	her	what	there
out	this	have	went
be	like	some	so
white	black	three	five
green	one	two	red

Connect For High Frequency Words
Wood End Stage 1

Game 3

blue	four	seven	yellow
six	eight	brown	ten
nine	pink	Monday	Tuesday
Sunday	Friday	Saturday	Thursday
Wednesday	day	twelve	days
purple	grey	orange	eleven

Also Available

The Wood End Series Stage 1

The Wood End Series Stage 2

The Wood End Series Stage 2 Teacher's Support Book and Precision Reading Programme

For more information about the author go to -

www.specialneedsconsultancy.co.uk

www.whatarespecialneeds.com